Awaiting Your Impossibilities

ANHINGA PRESS

Also by Donald Morrill

Poetry

With Your Back to Half the Day
At the Bottom of the Sky

Prose

Impetuous Sleeper
The Untouched Minutes
Sounding for Cool
A Stranger's Neighborhood

Awaiting Your Impossibilities

Poems
by
Donald Morrill

ANHINGA PRESS
TALLAHASSEE, FLORIDA 2015

Author photograph: Harry Johns
Design, production, and cover design: Jay Snodgrass
Type Styles: titles set in Sackers Gothic, body text in Adobe Caslon Pro

Library of Congress Cataloging-in-Publication Data
Awaiting Your Impossibilities by Donald Morrill — First Edition
ISBN — 978-1-934695-43-2
Library of Congress Cataloging Card Number — 2014957236

Anhinga Press Inc. is a nonprofit corporation dedicated wholly to the publication and appreciation of fine poetry and other literary genres.

For personal orders, catalogs, and information, write to:

ANHINGA PRESS
P.O. Box 3665 • Tallahassee, Florida 32315
Website: www.anhinga.org • Email: info@anhinga.org

Published in the United States by Anhinga Press
Tallahassee, Florida • First Edition, 2015

for Lisa

CONTENTS

ACKNOWLEDGMENTS

Arts & Letters: "Lives of the Poet"

Ascent: "To L"

     "The Untoward"

Blackbird: "Twenty-nine"

Colorado Review: "The Subdued Panelist at the Town Hall Meeting Realizes, Afterward, the Testimony He Should Have Given"

Hotel Amerika: "Passages to an Elegy"

Kestrel: "Now Is the Tampa of All Tampas"

The Massachusetts Review: "You, there, listening …"

     "You Get to Hold"

     "To L, After Parting Again"

     "Enemy Infant" (Winner of the Anne Halley Prize)

Many Mountains Moving: "Passing Through Char"

Mead: The Magazine of Literature and Libations: "Night's Here Again"

The Pinch: "The Intimate"

Prairie Schooner: "Love Might Utter the Only Verse That Wouldn't Insult the Dying"

TriQuarterly: "Late in the Anger"

     "Infinite Justice" (as "Poem of Infinite Justice")

AWAITING YOUR IMPOSSIBILITIES

First, birth, the break in oblivion,
Then a thousand ruptures in waking,
Then the call of one to another:
Day, what's your gift? Night, give me back!
I await your impossibilities!

ANOTHER CLEARING

The daisies close at evening   Crows have marched among them
Now you come

Look up   The tall cedars point to the center of night

The crow's scarlet mouth   The crow's famous intelligence

Now you stand with your chin as high as your ears
and no cry

Throats are cut among the satellites
but a man dreams of the crow larger than himself —
to elude it

He tries to make the daisies sing:
People live as though they were only souls

And the resinous dark smells faintly of caramel

At noon you can see nearly everything surrounds it

Crawl now   just a moment along the truth

LATE IN THE ANGER

I wake on this path   of this path   supine beneath swaying fronds

the woman watching me and over me   wondering at our fled cities   our myriad parents younger now than we   at the little we eat with our minds

The map will say we have driven ten thousand years to get here but there are no years in praise

and she has never slept and can finish no dream   Around us the pin oak leaves lie scattered   cupped and brittle as chitin

And my poor reason like a jowly man's black and silver reflection obliterated by his sudden water in a toilet

And the largest self like a worm writhing each time against the hook's barb

With my own mouth she insists   *You must be forgiven by the facts of this life*

And our secret goes out secret from us and returns in the finches jitting branch to branch   only so high and so low   through their habit of long succession

THE INTIMATE

Whose near miss are you, spouse of the murderous day, cousin of the rubble, citizen of the melted mirror? What struggles approach you from another city stricken? Do you, too, guess the smallest oblivion is mighty? We look on, though life shouldn't have to wake itself this way. Before justice sought words, it entered time as a scar. Who puts a hand to its shadow now, against the vengeful mind?

      Moth and flame: I am one —
      Idea and watcher;
      Brooder, sayer.

      Moth and flame: I am done —
      Smolder in flutter,
      Surface in layer.

      I am started: moth from flame —
      Nothing to alight,
      Death's circling betrayer.

      I am parted: flame from moth —
      Stillness through flight,
      Darkness out of prayer.

To survive the old sayings, their causes devour them.

Why weep for the horizon gone under the wrench? When frank, we know how to look at ourselves in the mirror. Like a bodiless wing, a leaf flutters in a web. Berries fall, clacking like raindrops, snapping like a bonfire.

And we step out the back door into bird shadow flowing from branches purple and bitter green.

You lift your face toward what you don't know. Do you hope to rid yourself of ecstasy in an average hour?

Remember, the good splinter teaches concentration. Were we so wise in being broken off, we would make no love but embody it.

Love the world?
        Eat the cell.
        Milk the wolf.
        Turn away.

World to love?
        Waves to name.
        Tick to pluck.
        (Now. Now.)

God would write a check if it would help them.

Pick up a pebble. Let it fall from your hand. Consider the road fleeing least of all underfoot.

Between its horizons, taste the acrid grayness smooth and jagged: pebble-heart, pebble-mind.

Look upon bitterness, that man sleeping in a dry well. He dreams he's an oasis and you a train of nomads lined up to drink from his hands.

Do you need to wake him to his narrow sky? You who had a pebble to toss at him, an earth.

    Woman says herself around a man.
    Man envelops nothing with his fist.
    He speaks peace, dares to call it woman,
    And woman says herself around a man.
    What does peace say to the broken hand?
    Undo the fates, that you were ever kissed?
    Woman says herself around a man:
    Man envelops nothing with his fist.

Pity: milk poured over ashes.

The lamp by which I write this — made by a prisoner of conscience?

To take up a pen under this small sun, one finds too easily he can't be good; barbed wire points as much outward as in.

It's so. Our truths won't staunch the sliced corners of honest mouths. I'd like this lamp to be only a lamp, mindless, on my side of silence.

I have a mouth that keeps from me.
I have a world not mine to stay.
I have a small pile posing as my house,
A blind to raise to the morning blossom.

I fall away from things, toward feeling
And scramble back to what? As what?
I have an error that's my breakthrough.
Mutinies — what else can love expect from us?

Hello, shy vein. Hello, frayed skirt.
Welcome, clank of the dropped doorknob.
There's muscle in the rapids yet, and luck —
A charm that never turns into us.

I have a terror that sweetens touch.
I have a freedom that schemes and scabs.
I have my death in another's dream
And time the form no thing abandons.

Patience: rain beating the lapels.

Subtle heart, fickle hammer, what's your reason? You hang on a nail, the rusting hook, your creation.

You clutch, pull out. You philosophize in bruise blood. How much pig iron in your forging!

Little tool of resignation, are you the missing beat? Little runaway, chipped, from making the neighborhood good.

Subtle driver, brooding lover, fighting sleep, fighting stillness. From others to others, we hear you breaking up a distance.

> To the scrabbling inside the wall
> That wakes him in the night, he whispers
> *I had a mother once, as well.*
>
> At the laughter like a baying stray
> New to the pound, she mutters
> *I was lucky my story ran away.*
>
> Beneath the wind chime cut from conduit,
> Silent, unconsoling, they wonder
> *How can I make no more of it?*

With all its living eyes, world can't behold itself.

YOU GET TO HOLD

You get to hold Lisa twitching through dream, you
get to hold what she can't remember — no matter
how many fly-bitten acolytes, borne
to ancient teachings sequestered in sorrow,
try to cure disillusionment with greater
disillusionment. The courageous murderer
may burn his way into the future
nightmares of survivors, but you're allowed to leave
the gifts given in rage, the yellowed pities,
beside the charred walls of just causes;
you're allowed to forget true and false still exist
and that life isn't simpler then but labors differently.
Fear may be the oldest part of us, lonely
with the dogma claiming now is *Monday, 3:14 a.m.*,
but you — you're also possessed of as much peace
as the generations in an inch of limestone,
and might be a little thankful not to see
a pietà in each kindness, and to think no question
beauty stays though every beauty fades. Stay awake
a while longer, then, to her hip against your hand;
hear the obscure summary in her next breath —
only a god suffers with understanding,
and you're spared that trouble now. Be still.

TO L

— This morning will take some song.

Long ago, life wrecked the dark's perfection. And that perfection can return, though words pass through us now like light through a leaf,

and one has to imagine each thing like a kissed face. Butterfly wings: eyelids of the dead
that flutter open

in a daydream —
a flight that makes one wince … Vanishing doesn't tell the truth longer. Nor

the next day with its wobbly table at the filling station where self-servers pump their own. The lover's sorrow hovers

like a glass globe above a spike, treasuring within it a fragrance. Does anybody really think their touch will send it plummeting,

shattering a prison? On the other side of an opened window, night is smaller than the fear of those who veer among its corners. Time rains on each place

and the moments pool where? If we could understand the existence, say,

of just nine frogs staring from a rose … we who ruin the body's limits (so lamented and inspiring) …

The waters rise through waters, sink through waters …

It's not accurate to say we take the fury that diminishes us, that it mixes with the dirt-caked fingers stuck in childhood's mouth. The meanings of human life are never disappearing, only disappearing for us who can't change with them.

We study, but who can prepare for the cores turned inside out, for our own shadows

plunged into rapids yet remaining?

A CAUSE OF THE PAST

— Rome, Second Century AD

When the aged slave Melbrotus lifts the vial of clear water,
his young master attends for the first time: *Here is your soul,*
and here the cry is widest, though you will not hear it. Imagine a love seat
too snug for sunlight. Imagine the nodding rose in evening hail,
destiny arranged by separate towels: for the hands, face, genitals.
The housefly, too, will understand without your permission;
and the round administrator with sweetened breath, and the demons unslain
but silenced by sacrifice never to be mentioned — you will be visible to them, as well,
though not as you may be to yourself, perhaps just once, mortified
by the obvious. Pour it out? Try. There is one, always, to congratulate
your death. The hive founded in the broken trough comes to hold it together.
And the modesty dependent on renown, the documents that turn, finally, against you —
all quenching, all begetting thirst. Each escape escapes …
Go now, transparent and of every color, you. Get to your lessons.

PASSAGES TO AN ELEGY

Whose leaf tumbles to the turtle's back? Who massages the beloved's neck and takes the census of the night clouds? Who doubts the prayers as they're recited? Who fishes the stocked pond?

The elation of shitting behind a dune in summer twilight, of putting a soul in order, all the thought knocked down to self-hatred or self-love — whose memory can we invade, whose should we really end?

In the shallows, a split branch grafts to its tremulous reflection. The dead say anything to please us now. They pause as we go onward — until we notice they've vanished from our side.

Weed, meet house.
House, meet wind.
Wind, meet vista.
Wall, meet thought.

Between these, we live.
No more small talk.
No vows. Between these
our fates, just that.

How long will death be interested in you? I try to stop the word, but stopping, too, begets. The leash sprawls on the porch, the house vacant.

I'd like to meet the raven's raven. I'd like the clarity of an icicle, the white vein — vision? — spinning down its core; time to study the new tooth, that wasp's nest in the palm frond, that mother face.

Clever shadow, you swing wide of me.
Have you never felt the skeleton love?

Stupid shadow, which way is freedom?
Hide beneath my heel, almost.

No looters, no impromptus, no salt-stained waders, no abolished fashions, no white rain, no sucker punch:

without our failing, without our filing, brawling, subtlety, grossness, calm won't be torn by the pick of human suffering.

No envy of screes, no weeping for true feeling, no policed bread, no spider web likened to a thumb print on air ... :

should the void screw through each mouth at last, should the thousand still intersections of a house connect nothing — is the interrogative simply bound elsewhere?

In the hand, the slap;
in the slap, the ocean;
in the ocean, the proverb,
in the candle, the focus:
the wick burned brittle
like the man in ice;
the ice around the man
like the day, tomorrow.

    Ridiculous body,
    break, pretend;
    unsigh your fate;
    the wild sleeps.

In flattery, the flea;
in the flea, the keystone,
in the keystone, inhibition;
in the looter, the promise:
the baby needing lies
like the breast and song,
the song bearing truth
like the neck bared to joys.

    Pitiless body,
    gather, hold.
    Don't turn us out.
    Don't provoke time.

That hand, newly-dead — take a picture of it if you like. It won't object if you think it resembles alabaster. Is it most your father's hand, or your mother's? Hands are hills, are evening. You waited for it to surprise you with the end, but the end eludes. Remember that caress, a flash across the face pink even in coma: a yellowing, the temples sinking … then the start of that most patient stillness. Lean in and *snap!* Cover the bandage with the sheet. *Snap!* Do relatives disapprove? Do you glance at their revenge? Art is "madness made marble," yet what logic keeps you trained on that compliant hand — *snap! … snap!* — and not its face?

Bitter laughter: the mirror snapped in two.
Which portion is offered to redemption?

Part with part of the reflection? Not all ours,
though we're too weak for silence.

The bereaved one irons tears into the shroud. Behind a bronze plaque, crickets sing of it. The blossom disappearing there said you'd know what to do with it.

INFINITE JUSTICE

Laugh   The jaws of the drugged tiger equal the sage friendless on her brilliant point

Wind batters the tents   awakens the one who peers out for the storm but sees stars only

What seems the final fruit will be the measure of harbors and flattery

Behind each wound is a wound that echoes *From where has this world escaped*

Money passing through iron bars   aches into platitudes   the joy pushing up to each body

Because your innocents were slaughtered your monsters will be honored for a hundred years

Because you touch a stranger and your touch comes back in his   how ignorant and skillful   it's lonely in the present and we come late to life

The jigsaw puzzles in hospital waiting rooms   The companies audited by daydreams

Foam flakes from the breakers   tumbles through the dunes   shards of white styrene

Will this roadside stone be thrown by aimlessness   Will mercy be pulled without the root

Because the afflictions are told by others who did not suffer them again and again as they prosper

because the dead are uninstructed   miserable in triumph   failed at praise

the apothecary's chimes ring in the March breeze   The age shines its pipe   rubbing the bowl along its nose

Laugh please   A sound wave becomes wood grain becomes shade and knotted fire   a dimple on a pond   from below

TO L, AFTER PARTING AGAIN

The long draw of trembling   Brink in the kiss   And the heretic's thrill —

Days like ball bearings in a bag burst on the floor —

The smaller windows opened   The deep tuck of the hammered nail   Bait shop in the mist —

Love-life   That it could be called that   Smell of stubbornness cut down   Wants to be said between atoms —

Unbeknownst me among unbeknownst you —

Seasons crinkling the sap   Curses left out in the dunes   Swindle in the mirror —

That it could be called that   Marriage of true minds —

We're not leaving it alone   The centuries wound adventure and animals embody great themes —

We must be broken into going   Must be bowls brimming into one another —

Gray sheen of sky on the damp earth road   And the depth furthered in front of each face —

THE SUBDUED PANELIST AT THE TOWN HALL MEETING
REALIZES, AFTERWARD,
THE TESTIMONY HE SHOULD HAVE GIVEN

You're breathing one of the atoms Alexander exhaled when he ordered the heads of thirty thousand stuffed on pikes

to teach his next foe meekness …

one from Marie Curie in the lab at midnight … one from Stephen Foster dying at thirty-eight, thirty-eight pennies in his pocket …

Then there's the breakfast rice sticky enough for tasting texture, the human meal, and the Beijing man inscribing on a raw grain one scene from *A Dream of the Red Chamber:* the maiden admires her single self in the hand mirror and turns it over to meet the image of her skeleton. That grin is magnified by the helpless glass declaring:

be amazed at what detail in so small a world.

A donkey brays to the night, staked down by the foreleg. Power lines buzz, just beyond your house? Imagine

the legless man on the Turfan-Kashkar bus, rolling smokes out of newsprint for the aged driver … and the two Chinese soldiers walking hand in hand near the rail yard, that gesture meaning

what?

Imagine, too, the knife the boyfriend brought to the rendezvous,

that surprised his ex-girlfriend who'd aborted their last link, thinking the way people clinging to the future think: this is the last time I'll need to see him.

She shouted. It didn't save her. It didn't save him from throwing himself afterward into the first oncoming fender. Yes,

the sticky rage of the witness, congealing between clumsy fingers, the mind dipping into the issue, to comfort the unknown. You

who may have once let a tear trace down your back its thick mineral history — this all adds up to something. Printed on wallpaper: butterfly after butterfly, identical, recurring. And Myth, that courtesan, ties knots in her sari,

only she can undo. Deep are those wood grains

beside the man at your dinner who, coming down hard, once held his pistol to a peasant chin and whispered *score me some!* The propeller and the lovely limb fit together again and again,

the torn city and the cleavage down which the drop of sweat went trying to make you come twenty years ago, and you did come … Are you trying still to follow it?

So much inside of time we can't behold — like a golden hound blanketed by hummingbirds. Tonight, as another lie is shouted through the voting, and the silent back rows go unrecognized, think with me

on the confession extracted from broken ribs, on the feelings that have no right. Consider the bougainvillea reddening windows across our region until it bursts like a heart within the heart —

and why, why it doesn't keep us from ourselves.

LOVE MIGHT UTTER THE ONLY VERSE
THAT WOULDN'T INSULT THE DYING

With each other, let's be simple.
        Place a blossom on the tongue.

With each other, let's be ample.
        Shut that history without a mark.

Let's be humbled like all temples.
        Fire tugs the air around us.

With each other, let's not gamble.
        Let's hold back, this time, from *Fairness*.

A tangled string of keys. And their locks? Ants ignore the stale trap, streaming toward some cryptic sweet.

Don't sit with me. Don't let me argue further. Leave me to the ink bottle and the morning mowing men, their necks studded with sweat-fed pimples, barking instructions over full-throttled motors.

Leave me to the stratagems of sinister confessors — self-improvement!

Get on through your best work and forget us until nightfall.

The gladioli droop.
Out they go!
Their murky, malodorous water!

No mourning our transience in theirs,
though they nonplussed us,
blazing in the farmers' market bin.

Remember when doubting my love for you,
for anything, proved
our passion was intelligent?

Your face withdrew into unbroachable darkness —
as though down a well, or mythic cave —
yet remained
untroubled as we spoke.

We must take our nerve elsewhere.

That man on the beach flying the two-inch kite
pulled from a cigar tube:
he's our muse.

And that tire tread along the sand
like the spine of an ancient fish:
a fossil
until the next wave.

The hour can't say how it becomes a day, a day a life, those gestures that are ours, not ours to observe only.

Love might countenance our gift, if we have one. We might hold its body in the night and thus the darkness. We might turn around at last and see that this is what the forgotten looks like, though we are not yet forgotten — ever taught, ever groping, crowd of ourselves in the gold wind.

The rose opens to our room tossed by loving.
It forgives us jobs we've had to part for.
What does it know about care before clippings?
Beneath the slot, mail sprawls — silence without us.
We've caressed the python at the children's zoo.
We've swum in rain, the old *us*.
We keep our dalliance with perfect solutions.
The rose craves tact, its radical priest
executed by partisans and resurrected by rhetoric.
We overthrow its piety, overthrowing ourselves.
Who can tell? We dressed like mortals and drove away.

LIVES OF THE POET

the grand life —

Rainy season. Doors swollen. Albany Avenue, Tampa, Florida.

The day's first drops, laurel leaves shiver like a horse's flank …

"The oldest form?" replies Tim the biologist, beside his martini on our porch. "A cloud … probably shaped like a paisley."

the unemphatic life —

Resting on the floor, the chair is wedded to the walls and ceiling, complacent as they dare not be about outer elements. Because the ceiling feels your weight below, it turns its worst face to the sky. Notice how the lamplight checks the random crack with shadows.

Whatever you have righted, and mistaken, will pass like clouds that only closing eyes can see. Whomever you have loved will orbit like a comet in the force of your elliptical memory.

This room and all the voids it pretends to keep in, keep out … Go ahead. Sit. A tension holds it together.

the evocative life —

"Scrotum flesh," says Lisa, tugging between my thumb and index finger. Three hundred million years ago, *Meganeura* swooped and darted, a dragonfly with wings as broad as the hawk snatching that dove from our power line yesterday.

What we take in is not the dark but the side of things turned away. To describe and not be described, to wish and not embitter — as a boy I searched for memory until everything became a memory, a dove in the talons, twisting to free itself.

Lisa's pink hands tinge the water in the white basin. The grit on the oranges still ripening in our tree resembles the night side of planets.

the lofty life —

This twig did not appear soon enough to become a trunk and so has no regrets about the unachievable. It seemed destined to fall, so much so that falling is the true beginning of what it might call, joking as it does, "the life of a failed sparrow perch."

Parched and, thus, seasoning, it will abide far below the daily gusts — there in the swaying shadows. It will never snap under paw or foot, never warn prey or extend a hunger, never inspire — as it could with its rueful tales of ruinous mites — a campfire.

To inscribe in the dirt so long surrounding it a map of the home country, a treasure map, any figure to please a dreamer — when it imagines what it would take to be a magic wand, a silly scepter, this is all it learns to hope for, in its allotted hour, from its place on Earth.

the grave life —

Night lifts my silvered chin as if to say *Your love is dear but just a crush.*

Lightning shakes me out of sleep. There's a shower, no heavier than a crumbling negligée — enough to bring the smell of earth.

Who's stronger than a crack, a ripe berry, sorrow rights?

the polished life —

Maybe it's a great sadness, that whiskey breath, one among the other blue suits passing in the atrium at ten a.m. I push myself through the revolving door, so I can think that atmosphere might whisper a secret joy in hating, a confident repulsion at all one had acquired in plain sight. Success then might lie in fiery spirit, drowning some ice, rebellion composed of two parts pleasant dizziness, one failing mint.

We often bless ourselves this way, in the presumption of another's suffering and our good luck. The day before me makes no comment, but the light cuts as though I'd stepped into it from bar shadows.

I squint at the brief pain of being, and the revolving door sucks and gasps. Then on to my appointment, nodding to Giddiness and Fear, those two onlookers, the leashes on their pets entwining as they talk.

the ornate life —

Obsessive, destitute monologues on politics. Germane, obstinate intrigues with the self. Historic revelations, strategic retractions. Arraignments, enticements, mêlées , scoldings, drubbings, rehearsals — and all before brunch!

I close my eyes to reach more precisely behind horizons. These same eyes squeeze out their sexual vintage. But, see, on your hat brim now, a grasshopper minus one back leg …

Why argue further about our tastes in gods? Or how what was truly ours would leave us for its destiny. Why try again to brush paint onto childhood ponds? I'd like to hear you as a singer — one who begs the tune: Flesh, don't leave me behind!

the refined life —

Waking, Lisa growls as she stretches. In a Budgetel parking lot, she dances to Glinka, doors open to the car radio. I take snapshots of her from the balcony, a dead roach in the corner of my viewfinder.

You know the proverb *Laughter may retire to the more stable molecules, but we come after ourselves.* Was it Glinka? We've searched but haven't found that melody again.

"None of the works of those ancient heretics survive," says Jane the historian, years later, beside the lantern on our porch, "We know them only by the writings of their enemies."

the vigorous life —

Why fear the conventional? Become robins swarming ripe berry bushes, shattering violet skins, juice burning to the tips of careening, colliding wings.

White and purple cosmos gawk, one blossom among you bearing four petals of each color — as the botanists say: incomplete expression …

Thrilled differently from the first time, bring shadows to each other. Bloom. Pick. Sway on your manifold limbs.

the pregnant life —

During the heaviest downpour, three honey-brown droplets well at a crack in the ceiling plaster. Still, ten thousand nests of exterminated mud-daubers cling beneath Morris Park Bridge.

Certain beauties speak so flesh falls from the bone. And the final cries to those from our first moments? They linger, near the finding side of the soul.

Again, I take up an acorn for what we might yet have — minnows to be approached without our shadows scattering them. I leave this tribute wrongheaded but necessary.

the spontaneous life —

Even a cup of coffee has a soul that you can never call back, though you'll want to seek who you are in who you were the day you drank it, thinking nothing then but what the recent office coup might mean for aspirations so clear to you and no one else, clear and contrary to a certain whisper in your daydream ear.

That whisper convinced you those hopes must be driving you toward a way more apt to beat back the timidity in aging, your one-man trend toward fleeing the "great work" that makes existence worth all the years have claimed it must become against pointlessness.

It's elusive work, this defining, formed by bitterness futile and dull if allowed to rule like a despot whose intelligence derives from spies and a murderous murdered mother rising from his sleep, and the song of a shepherd boy he heard once while carried on his throne to battle.

the exquisite life —

Don't look into these eyes. They've closed on stars, confused dawns and dusks. They've caressed intimate signatures. But when they turn toward you, they're blinded by tears withheld.

They've spoken rashly, entranced by the distance your embrace has traveled. They want to be known like hands cupping weights for measuring ore.

Your light banishes the void I despise and cling to. You're the muscling spirit in the sail. Where shall we go in each other's sight? If you look into these eyes, it's the world again.

the artless life —

This time, I'm not cursing the sailboat's mast passing through the raised drawbridge I should have already crossed. I'm not wincing at the thought of Lisa's ire when I arrive at the beach late. I don't care if she won't read Lorca to me in the Spanish, as she's promised for weeks.

The surroundings here gather slowly around me, wildlife returning to a path. Sunlight rubs the watch dial I strapped to my wrist, getting ready.

How my father waited for the call, his mother dying. He steered through three hours, thinking of the last thing to say, then held her hand in silence.

the untrammeled life —

Grieve for the loss of this moment, for the way you failed to live it. Imagine your inability to embrace it fully. Then you are beginning to approach happiness.

Everything is escaping you — that, too, is happiness. The arroyo you stood in for five minutes one summer twilight five years ago, that beautiful but dull moment revisiting you with its purple glory as you make the last turn into the parking deck (always at this turn, never elsewhere) — that, too, is happiness, a few molecules transformed by all that has happened to you and now ending as a surprise, a little sweet chime that vanishes as quickly as it cheers you.

Here, too, you encounter the flicker of an uncatalogued species swooping on its wings back into branching shadows, a secret happiness that hardly has to do with your condition, your general state, yet lives with you, breathing. It knows you are there, even if you don't know it exists.

the well-knit life —

Imagination: the several husbands of a widow wishing for a marriage that can last her.

In grief, in wonder, in embarrassed amusement at each loss (not every one through death, but one surmised from a lengthy disappearance and another faked until it held enough separation to be true), she finds that suitors come to those who do not tend their gardens but own the cash register, chair a council, and relent just enough at dinner.

Matronly, she cups the cut-glass bourbon, with her current muse in his suspenders now, seated on the porch swing, believing he's the one and only.

the distinctive life —

This age is a traveler's broken candle, a revolution's flag become a bedspread. This age is *34 Must-See Looks for Spring!* And Cesar's karaoke tonight at Snack City.

A xeroxed ass. Black market cornflakes. Imagine, your own skull become a gilded drinking cup!

Fred lays newspaper across his yard, spreads dunes of mulch over the scandal and hue. A thorn from the vine entangled in our common fence breaks off and sinks into the whorl of my right thumb. We wave to each other, talk. With a red-hot needle cooled to blue, I probe. He snatches at weeds that break through buried words.

the devious life —

Here the leaves don't reach up and clap the moon differently than elsewhere, nor do treble clefs swirl in the stream uniquely. Our bodily confections still toss love at the dire, somewhere down the hill beside the horse graves. We've just quarantined ourselves from summer rental remedies for loss.

Advice is ecstatic sadness — spilled wine unnoticed by the spiller turning people into hugs. No hangovers, these days, no insistence we've found a form before phoniness — just this invitation.

The lupine never blunders, and we're here with no more reason than to draw and see. So what will it be — dodging tastefulness and other last resorts there in the city … or the genius of the season we might bring together? Dragging out the silhouette that Mother called to at the end … or the black fly's bite?

the natural life —

Recovered from tar pits, Dire Wolf skulls hang on the museum wall, row upon row, all muzzles aimed to the right as you face them, eye sockets still surprised, it seems, by what has caught them.

They remind me of a vision, years ago, in a winter market: breath pouring out of each body there and vanishing, out and vanishing, reappearing to go from one of us to the next, to the next.

Those skulls, those breaths: alike yet ruthlessly various. I'd forgotten how cold I was among strangers, hungry for the flesh on the vender's striping grill. I'd figured my place among coins the flesh trades, the coin of the moment I had to pay and paid — mine still, until now.

the vivid life —

More than one is tempted to flee by shouting inwardly *Names on headstones — more time ahead than behind!* More than one is tempted to pretend: Tear apart Ever and find berries at the roadside you didn't see before, those with the dull finish riper and sweeter than the glossy. More than one is tempted to beg *Day, what's my task?* One, from the bulk barrel of gestures … One, among the best bones illusion can steal … How can I admit *I* when a branch runs beneath it?

Where hands have crossed this life: a beginning to look into. Spirit is a helpless kiss for that face within a face … And *soul* a hapless reaching for the jar of knocked-out teeth smashed on palace steps by guardians of the silenced. Don't tell me you don't see it. Human, like a debt. "Write something funny," Lisa pleads, "just once, and not be native …"

Me? Ruthless in sitting, of the untuned, pimpled and bold? The present twists and scrams … and wakes up to find itself still here, needing to go on. Who has more than one story? Who tells it quickly and is done? Who hides the dénouement from friends, to keep them? Who pauses, begs the interruption?

the poignant life —

An ancient guild killed one of its enemies and avoided prosecution by having each member take a bite. At another gathering, the distinguished guest pleased himself most of all, saying, "We talk about the speed of sound and light, but what about the speed of suggestion?"

Now honey locust blossoms flutter down on the alley no one regards. See them behind the eyes? Now a false alarm sobs down Albany Avenue in the unmade film *A Clear Day and No Memories, Part II*, its tears for property evaporating.

Where is the question which is itself a caress? "You live as much as you can," says old Dorothy, against the retirement facility, "and die when you can't help it."

the transcendent life —

Among the sparkling phosphorescent plankton, beyond the moonless breakers, our friends gleam and brighten as they swirl along the surface. They darken as they grow still and let themselves sink.

"We've got to stay for dawn," one says. "Yeah," says another, "you rarely get this water." And I agree, getting a mouthful, tasting the salt to remember this by.

Then a light touches mine. "You're it!" And I look around. Only stars on black swells. Yes, we finally came to the rented house, carrying each other's clothes.

the ethereal life —

A man on his bed, regretting his mouth, wincing at his shame and wondering at its source; a man returned to failure: a stick jammed into a fish eye, a shattering like downed pine trunks bursting with spring ice.

He sleeps … and leaps back to a place that sheltered him so often (a grotto? a garden?) …

He steps through its floor suddenly rotten, farmhouse walls silvered with abandonment.

the light-hearted life —

Lisa among butterflies beside the deadly falls — honey yellow, white, orange, Chinese scarlet: on the fine muscles of existence, a thousand leaves refusing to fall just once.

Our calves tremble from descending switchbacks, under vultures on switchbacks of air. We eat our candy bar and dried berries. We told the bathers at the well far above we had no food. They'd asked for bread, giggling shyly.

The bite welts on my hands — we could have kept on leaning at a resort table on the peak, or swinging out on the roped seat there hung from a swaying branch. (The wind lifts you daydreaming dusty roads to the pass.)

the flowing life —

First day of autumn, sprinkles on the hot tub. The poorly organized hurricane has turned away, as unpredicted. Our shelters have closed, evacuees bussed home. The dead tree felled in yesterday's blow lies across the neighbor's red hibiscus.

First day of first days … the mother of three kittens steps among the clearing puddles of Albany Avenue. So many twigs! Where's the cold deli from the hand that wants her fixed?

Put it out, she yowls, Come on, you and your hopes of catching!

NIGHT'S HERE AGAIN

Night's here again, Marcos, with Seville at the window.
Night in the squares where the good, crude jokes are born.

Shall we head out to hear the settled score against Real Madrid?
And Jose's excoriations of Franco and now the new fascists
(promenading discreetly with tasteful jackets over their shoulders)?

The Heart, too, Marcos, like eucalyptus in the drained moat,
like porch paint worn away by years of cat sleep,
and cigars hardening in the heat.

One look, tops, from that gang woman at the café — no more …

and that round boss in white coveralls yelling on the corner:
you've screwed down the manhole and left the goddamn part below!

Jacarandas, Marcos …
                And Pedro "the scholar" (because he lies) —
his florid style a rage at being born to plain people.

Again, dust from ancient friezes is rinsed from tourist hair,
the constipated one longing for the turtle to get off the bus!

Night's here, and the laughter and the cards.
An old man with no butt clawing a girl with his eyes.
And raw flounder on ice, gleaming like waxed terrazzo.

Do we go to the rattle of plastic awnings in the breeze?
Do we nag the flesh: *C'mon, steal us a form from the air!*

LINES AND EXPLANATIONS

The dreaming one claws uphill to that first house,
the streets there wadding in his hands like bed sheets.*

*(I woke and heard my wife online down the hall and remembered
having nothing more to say to my dead mother.)

This river stone has the flavor of certain childhood hours,*
part winter gloaming that memory doesn't brighten or clear.

*(Somewhere in *Getting Used to Dying*, Zhang Xian Liang has his narrator say, in translation:
"The side without power is always the side that is accused of being irrational.")

O Fossil Nothing, collect yourself.
Be gone, Going. Be lost, Losing.*
I'm nothing, too, but not like you.
I was started — though who believes that?

*(Tom's sister asked him: "What's with this tone of yours, like confetti blowing from a morgue?")

The cormorant dips its head again into the surf —
like a needle leading unknotted thread.*

*(Near Ft. Madison, Iowa, a hillside had been mowed in the shape of Mickey Mouse. At the center of it stood a memorial wreath.)

You can lift yourself from that
want that pit that wail

you can float and try to float*

where you come to
rest at last
will be destroyed

*(The combat medic, his hand red from the wound, held up the armor-piercing slug to the reporter: "When I told you I do not let people die on me, I meant it.")

ENEMY INFANT

The red coals pouring into the infant's mouth
No
The infant's mouth in the raider who pours

No the mother gagged and forced to witness it
Then raped and shot the milk of her murder

No
The coals of revenge and the clans of clarity
The separatists the occupiers the old seeking wise silence

The infant's father staring out from whetted blades
The widower waiting tables for the nation of his exile
No

The infant grown up see how tall the night marching
See the gangs ground into rebels to season distant headlines
Azaleas bursting from palace barricades No

No only the infant
The infant and its wail was there ever such a peace

MONTEVERDE

— (Costa Rica)

The wind here may teach you the shapes of staying. Gusts snap across a paused, sailing hawk — shaking inner windowpanes.

The wind here needs Januaries, a cloud to tear, Sojourner. The split needs a branch, fresh you.

*

Cloud-fall swirling like dust in sunlight. Will your life take you back, when you want it?

You who come to view a mile-long vine, to poach a golden toad, a stone leaned two years against the co-op's side door. Where have the other stones held?

*

Then the wind flees town, in the night, before it's found out. Bees appear. Bananaquits perch. Hear it? The hammering at Moon Shiva.

You mistook the season. How does it feel to be treated as a lover? May these words, like a scorpion, be made up in that bed.

*

Under one leaf wonder roosts as a bat
Under one leaf hums a gentleman with baston
Under one leaf governments pretend
Sex is ambiguous, as are thoughts
       save those in green
Sky's jealous of one leaf's other side
       still of the earth

Roots long for that prominence as unearned as beauty
One leaf that falls never falling
          from the secrets

*

Footsteps behind you, on the night path, alone: the white horse there, fearing you.

Stones know their future's in breaking, in smaller. The horse knows its way home.

*

The wind here returns to the thick hair of the poor, the thorn fitted perfectly to each blow.

Cloud-fall rushing, arcing, in sunlight.

At the end of that rainbow stands a flatbed truck.

IN MEMORIAM

Should we suffer   what face can the air have

What imploring

Should we vanish   who

Who do you remind

Of whom do you remind them   refused in themselves

Turn to the face in the leaves   the face larger than yours

The hearthstone alone beside an oak

Rain is worth mentioning   the face of mother in the clinic waiting room
Anger you must see because it can't be shown to death

The pastel paintings in the lobby   their beach breezes she'd gladly step into

Red coal   readiness   ripeness of wave crash

We stop talking to her
As we knew her and begin as she will be   what we think she will be

We're hurrying her to a stronger channel (more familiar)

Should she suffer   whose rain is worth mentioning

Should we   whose enemy does it defeat

(As though time could fall like a tree
Clutching stones with its roots)
(Tree that doesn't fall enough
Resting on its smaller neighbors)

What a plummet is an anniversary
What plumbs

— *A.M., d.9.5.03*

SEVILLE

Sadness has failed. The siesta trembles in certain beds,
 there's hide and seek, too, in the park below, and a drum roll.
"You're not from here" Lisa's hat brim sings
"You wear a hat like that only on a horse" (and we have no horse).
We have a man trying to conceal his wart with a sideburn,
 we have dumpsters brimming with broken pavement,
 and a little shop that sells only holy cords,
 and the lights of La Giralda blinking off into midnight.

Then you, Marcos, open our coin purse, *the Old Whore*,
 and sigh, "We'll go as far as she takes us,
 but she just keeps taking, she never tires out …"
 and, later: "Rafa, I'm not eating yesterday's bread."
We think we're traveling, but some façade cracks
 have meandered through centuries to get here.
The Archives of the Indies, the Murillo Madonnas —
 we pass them for Bar Jota, El Tremendo, El Rinconcillo
(where that dapper old man isn't alone nightly, as we'd guessed).

But that tourist there, poor bastard pilgrim! —
                                    he won't be duped
 by the picturesque: that possum-faced waitress,
 or the swallow nests beneath eaves (pests!);
 the kiss in the park? — he smiles ruefully at it,
 as though it reminds him of something:

a TV show … or the experience I might have had
(should have had) at eighteen, had I been less selfish
and more courageous —
                              But where was I?
or we, really, who like to hear our heels in different towns?
Sadness had failed, Mopeds were running every stop light,
Bob Marley and Charlie Chaplin were quoted on sugar packets …
and, you, Lola, still making Marcos wait two hours
in front of the wedding office twenty years ago —
"My hair wouldn't stay up!" you told him
as you tell us now, grinning over breakfast snails.
That girl's come home in you, no? — to her widowed mother
with the new bidet and the niece skipping school
to sell bootleg CD's for her gypsy boyfriend.
She pours more wine each time we think
finally (really) we know how to live …

Put a cathedral here, a martyrdom there,
and we begin to get the crumbling cork.
The driver silent until asked about his taxi,
ripping onward right away with "Each morning,
I look in the mirror and say 'This rice is overcooked.
But, okay, work to live not live to work, right?'"
The Old Whore tips him. "As pedantic as mother's milk,"
Marcos groans, a gobbet of black yarn drifting
twelve floors from a balcony, down to the Moorish baths.

We think we're returning, I bet we're dreaming
somewhat together: Friendship, known by many names

like a god or a spice. This town birthed Lola *and* Trajan,
and we're hangovers who've earned their memories,
we have Marta growing a single white hair with her terrible twos,
we have the curved tip of the matador's final sword,
and the prized loneliness of fountains. "The water is shit,"
says the grocer, though it tastes of throbbing roses.

Then Rosa's laughter is the day talking. Remember,
Spaniards don't like their legs cut off in photos,
and Montesino's garden — a dirt patch along the river —
honors poetry as well as Machado's lemons
ripening behind the Duquesa's gates. Take consolation
from that shoeshine resembling the boss you left behind,
in that land of roaches as plump as these walnuts …
the championship, the masterpiece, the holy day
mean nothing beyond defining a few million lives …
and forget those updates on monastic self-improvement!
And the vaginal mouths of pond carp at Alcazar!

Bait and switch has failed. Adjourn to the sierra,
and there's the quaintly delirious sheen
edging La Nava's roofs at twilight, the stork nested
against the ancient, fragile steeple, unwilling to abandon
banging hours for that platform put up nearby.
                                        Gone already,
one might hear the lone, dry leaf clawing the square there: that life.
Out the window I fall and swoop off on a gray pigeon,
so I can back away from myself and meet a rescued sailor …

"If I don't see you again," José says, I've seen you enough,"
and Lisa wonders how he builds those towers in Madrid.
"The museums are free today," Isabel adds, "but we are full of ham."
Lola, will you translate? Or any of us? —
impaled on the hospitality of satirists …
We have the souvenir painter: all her portraits look like *her*,
we have Domi's great-grandfather murdered "by mistake" — with an ax,
and the pay phone blocked by flamenco,
and indolent breezes blurring reflected trees,
strewing golden blossoms. The man we ask
can't say what they're called. He just sweeps them up.

THE UNTOWARD

"Poor Man's Orchid" blows across the yards, scraggy purple blossoms "not native," out of weak wood …

And the girl with bells strung around her waist — that first girl —

she's come back from the Temple of Ishtar
in the guise of colliding dragonflies, the riffling of newspaper …

To stand behind the one on whom the kiss comes down, to put lips to the beautiful muscle —

could a spear have once flown here, a tumbrel's wheel turned over this hill? In the old poems, the gods filled the hero's heart with valor —

now *I so want to be about me* hums this noon, licking its paws, curled in the great slowness beneath parked cars …

Dub it Tuesday, the appetites preparing this world for themselves alone.
Dub it moralizing, with Reality
the heretic.

Down the I-4 median, a scruffy teen marches and spins, arms swirling in his gleam. On Pluto — I'm sure of it —

the small hard tears ground back into the eyes
congregate for a last write-off before they're shipped to galaxies less fortunate than ours.

People live as though they're far away and intimate. People live as though.

And isn't it fitting, Mr. Consciousness? Even as nails
pounded through a scapegoat's feet

hit nails driven through others hung on that cross,

you're not stuffing my ears with more tickets to paradise.

THE STUMP IN THE WELL

In the backyard of a tract house lapsed and abandoned,
a mock wishing well encircles a walnut tree stump.

Too much has occurred to learn where the lopped branches lie
(noon perchings and star grabbing and snow-loaded sleep);

no chemical analysis will trace that vanished stillness,
a shade not of limbs alone nor limbs alone to shape …

No writing up ruins here, no introducing myself,
nor working anyone out, nor lending a song to evil

(though who can track its harmonies and counterpoint-to-come?)
The stump's the thing and its tiered surroundings,

which join concealment to art. Why do we seek to save
only human things that happened on this spot?

Beside the mystery, our differences are slight,
though they compose the characters of our lives:

The tastes of walnuts in a bowl, changing as they gleam,
sweet meat in the memories of mouths open for the chance.

Some thoughts are picked unbroken from the black, acrid shells.
The dead say *forever* slowly, so we may understand.

NOW IS THE TAMPA OF ALL TAMPAS

La vida with everyone in it, someone's ninth town,
A thousandth home to luxuriant unpossession.

Of August noon casting down its powdery halo,
December light the thinnest pane of raw potato.

Week 35, Week 17, at the vanished timeshares,
stadium-roars in a plastic cup, tingling the fingers.

Now Mandarin faces in bedded pansies,
night gods twisting in the frangipani.

Traffic still knotting hours after
good news suddenly slows one driver.

A sparking rabbit rounds the dog track,
past the propeller works and yachts on blocks.

Waters so soft you can't shave close! Pink lightning!
In Council Chambers the motion still carrying.

Tampa of clacking pennants and spouses twined like driftwood.
Tampa the vast gut touched like a faraway wound.

Of graffiti scored on sea grape leaves,
divining lap dancers silvered with fatigue.

Future Nails   All Day Nails   Eternal Nails,
searing beach sand squeaking beneath the heels.

Tampa so alive no one can serve it truth,
shade offering itself like contraband fruit.

Those first books buried in the wilderness,
stilled bombers at the base, quartered Percocets.

Back and forth beneath table-top glass,
a tabby passes its paw, peering through, entranced.

PASSING THROUGH CHAR

A fallen live oak leaf resembles live oak leaves
yet is identical to none. The split vein, broken panel, color
determine this, as well as where each lands, O wind.
Convention underfoot that once reigned overheard. History
like the burning called *controlled*,
and the shadow it casts on trunk and branch
long after. Someone comes along and makes a note of it,
smells the day and remembers
nothing of this black and silver trail, this public tract
yet. The undergrowth is managed, thus,
without lightning or lightning gods.
Each step across the ash resurrects small bursts of smoke
and leads toward greener things.

LINES AND EXPLANATIONS (II)

The serpent's jaws now close around a cloud.*
How can people speak what they know?

                  *(James Richardson wrote: "Nothing is more real than what's impossible.")

Clumped oak leaves
rainwater and time
      can rot steel*

She put a blossom in his way
He put a blossom in her way

                  *(A hope doesn't grow less likely because you've sought its confidence.)

Woman in the alley night,
foraging through trash,
her little boy behind.
The poet smooths his verses.*

*(It was reported that the Russians aren't taking to Capitalism: "They don't wish their children rich but for their neighbor's cow to die.")

Moon: pearl that rises and drowns,
thigh scraped by heavy coins.
Soul: untried bitter goddess,*
graves dug to fool lost enemies …

*(A man on the second floor of the construction site raised his binoculars again as a woman stepped from the gym across the street.)

Late, drunk, tip-toeing not to waken her,
I look to see if there is rain* now in that wind.

*(As the subway doors closed, the man stood and declaimed *One day you're going to get it all and you'll be without and know what it's like … I'll rip your face off, motherfucker, What are you looking at? And where do you think you're going?*)

Among the many tongues of murder
each year kisses deeper.

The pup next door — hear that whine? — senses*
master going down on master.

*(In *The Undiscovered Country,* William Logan claims, "A belief is just a little stick you hang the
poem from.")

TWENTY-NINE

1) A blossom spirals outward over the meditating eye. Dog licks himself. Forgive. Dog sneaks onto his master's chair.

2) Purple rabbit's foot, why is there thought? Wind leans back in a rocker. No symbol fits a life.

   The futility of houses simply passing for houses …

3) The clock speaks to the horizon, the pigment to the keening, the ocean to the footprint, the reckless window to the stone —

   of the wilderness in law, of the casting off of futures, of the flowing in the granite, of the virgin deck of cards.

4) Now ten thousand time capsules lie buried world-wide. We walk between ourselves, with our bitter teachers and their wisdom. Love,

   your letters never finish me. That's our correspondence. Anything is possible but not everything.

5) Beneath the tripped-over, dislodged stone: a socket of black earth. A man repeats himself in different ways. Hear? On the other side of the wall, the *rake-rake* of a skater working up the hill toward Big View.

6) Is there a thinner, emptier thing than I

   craving to be the light around my shadow?

7) Pebble and moss on a bed of blued deadwood: each thing intricate, unique and general, combined admiringly —

yet a graceless wish,
missing sun and cloud, the god arrangement (mountainside).

8) Beauty comes to ash, morning light to ferns. Night teems with "What if?" Are you, too, stuck awake?

I split a green walnut: clear juice and milky meat, the odor of citrus. My love rolls on her back, her soles, to the sky, black with earth.

9) Her talk draws talk from me I can't draw from myself: When such wings are torn off,

friend, wings are granted.

10) Falling asleep, I startle awake — to stop my fall from the first tree. A million years pass in my opening eyes, though I see now my dead-father face.

11) Days without my lips touching hers, though we talk, we tease and argue. Loveseats in the park speckled with bird droppings. A girl kneeling on a skateboard in the street.

12) Where are you now, who lay across my shoulders like a plush fallen arras? You,

catastrophe. The elm doesn't mourn the grove that once surrounded it. In the channel, anchored ships are still leaves in the current.

13) We must treat each other lightly, lightly, one thinks, alone, under island pines, *We must, we are such weight.*

Now the candle flames all lean one way.

14) That hat. That lamp. That hidden ticket. Each object has its moment to cry out: *You've aged while I've aged, you've forgotten while I've remained, you don't know about knowing. Come back, dust, to me, the one thing!*

15) The tombs in the ground where archaeologists sought gold ... now refilled, brimming with gravel ... And I have all these fine emotions!

16) So puzzling and remote, the beauty of wisdom — the offered kiss ignored on the landing ... and at the Truth Commission hearing: laughter in the spokesman's gravity. See the bottomless record, the plummet of our funding ...

17) *Climb higher* says the moment. *Descend* replies the watch *and pack your things to leave.*

18) A speedboat in the pasture. Birds mating in freefall. Every god weaves.

Pity the poet whose poems have been loyal.

19) It's not your death I carry, love, but my idea of your death — which your death will strip from me should I live to meet it.

20) Twins greet a man between planes. One gets a kiss. The river, gray with filings, glitters in the clear morning. How can we not trust appearances?

21) Most of *us* is here in memory: the hurricane in a forest leveled, sawed for logs, cured or burned green.

22) Satisfaction? The tender hand loyal to here and here, the third superfluous coin, three peers and one superior acknowledging … Then comes sweet renunciation … and the hearts that could be ours: black, unquarried granite; an opened safety pin sewn into a jacket lining …

23) Says the roar in the cells, the baton in the mountain, the gold dust in the rampart, the hammock laced by vines:

Dignity should possess you like the wind its cherry blossoms falling into litter, lifting.

24) They throw their mattress into the pool. Out with old sex! They watch it undulate seductively, sinking, sinking … too still on the bottom.

25) I write a reasonable verse to acknowledge the unreasonable — the evil that flatters me in this ambition, the truths I miss to make my point.

Hear the voice from under the rubble? May it interrupt the muse.

26) The alchemists believed metal came from a seed, the desire for one thing to come from another.

A bare branch blocks no view with character. Four crows then perch suddenly upon it.

27) Slow-flying moth, so small, insistent — my fierce clap blows you free of harm.

28) Someone's talk and someone's silence: the shadow where the campfire stopped crawling along a twig.

29) Of the graft of *you* to *me*, of *now* to *there*, we believe you know all and try to tell. Thus your light, moon, and these balconies.

YOU, THERE, LISTENING

You, there, listening
for the poem to speak a truth
useful for the nights when one, surprised by a diagnosis,
lies planning his funeral through vengeful tears —
forgive it if it speaks of the gold dust of spring
seeding the laces of boots.
Poems are as impolite
as they are perceptive, as beside the point
as the actual. Their gold sticks to unsuspecting hands
tying and untying two ordinary knots
then grasping other hands and objects.
What else can we offer
but our secrets and their failed understanding?
The surprised one lies alone with his vision — forever.
He craves comfort, while the poem strives to imagine him
laboring to realize those knots will outlast him.
A poem's wilderness can make you mad that way.
So that, stuck with it,
you go to him, maybe,
and try to give what no poem can.

About the Author

Donald Morrill is the author of three volumes of poetry as well as four books of nonfiction. He has taught at Jilin University, Peoples' Republic of China, and has been a Fulbright Lecturer at the University of Lodz, Poland, as well as the Bedell Visiting Writer in the Nonfiction Writing Program at the University of Iowa and the Tammis Day Writer-in-residence at the Poetry Center at Smith. Currently he teaches in the Low-Residency MFA in Creative Writing Program at the University of Tampa and is Associate Dean of Graduate and Continuing Studies there. He is married to the writer Lisa Birnbaum.